PIANO
VOCAL
GUITAR

STEVE GREEN   THE ULTIMATE COLLECTION

D1610316

ISBN 1-4234-1097-1

7777 W. BLUEMOUND RD. P.O. BOX 13819 MILWAUKEE, WI 53213

Visit Hal Leonard Online at
www.halleonard.com

BROKEN AND SPILLED OUT

Words by GLORIA GAITHER
Music by BILL GEORGE

*Recorded a half step higher.

CHERISH THE TREASURE

Words and Music by
JON MOHR

EMBRACE THE CROSS

Words and Music by
JOHN G. ELLIOTT

22

Em - brace the cross, em - brace the

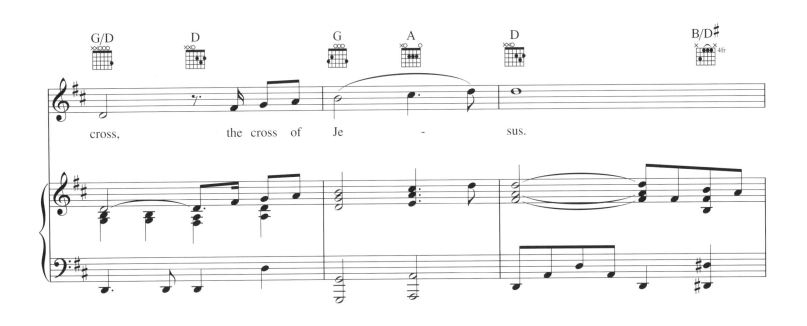

cross, the cross of Je - sus.

rit.

GOD AND GOD ALONE

Words and Music by
PHILL McHUGH

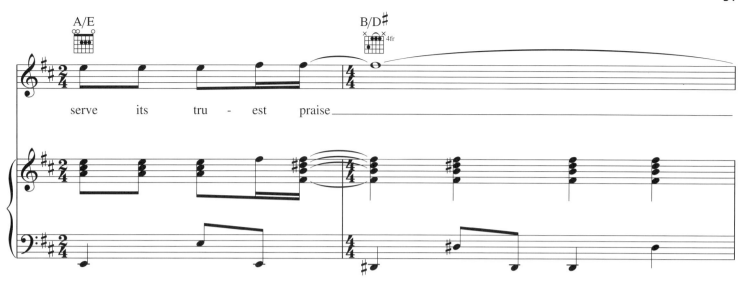

serve its tru - est praise

for God   and   God   a -

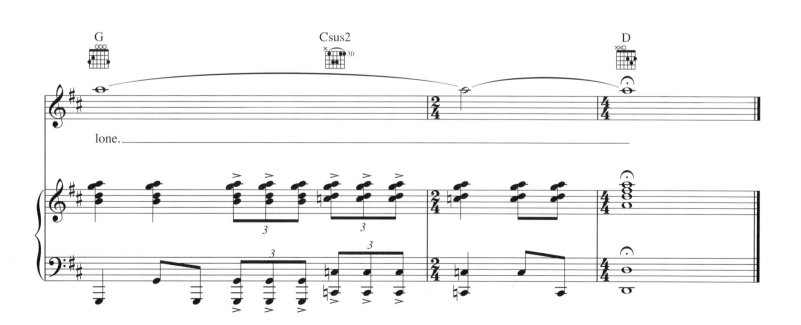

lone.

ENTER IN

Words and Music by STEVE GREEN,
GREG NELSON and JON MOHR

Slowly

Noth-ing chills the heart __ of men __ like pass-ing through __ death's gate; __ yet to
con-flict still con-tin-ues rag - ing deep with - in _____ my soul; __ the

him who __ en-ters dai-ly, death's a glo-rious fate. __ Dear-ly be-
Spir-it _____ wars a-gainst my flesh __ in a strug-gle for con-trol. __ My on-ly

THE FAITHFUL

Words and Music by MICHAEL CARD
and PHIL NAISH

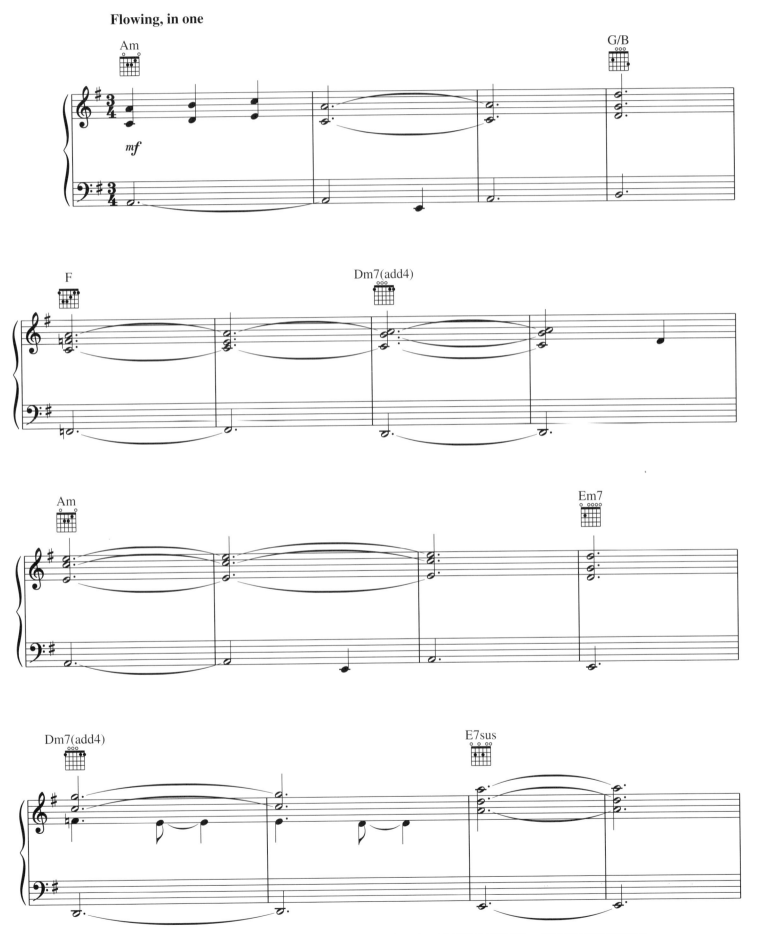

is the seed of the church. _____

The

How church. _____

long Lord? _____ How

is the seed

of the church.

rall.

FIND US FAITHFUL

Words and Music by
JON MOHR

pil- grims on ___ the jour - ney of the nar - row road, ___ and

50

GOD CAUSES ALL THINGS TO GROW

Words and Music by STEVEN CURTIS CHAPMAN
and STEVE GREEN

54

God caus - es all things___ to grow. _

HE HOLDS THE KEYS

Words and Music by
JON MOHR

Moderately

Death rides black-ened clouds a - cross the sky. The Son of man lays down to die. With

though we've been held cap - tive, ____ at long last we are ___

free for __ He holds _____ The Keys._

A -

HE IS GOOD

Words and Music by FRANK HERNANDEZ
and JEFF NELSON

He is good, He is good. His love en-dures for-ev-er. Give thanks to the

*Recorded a half step higher.

72

HE WHO BEGAN A GOOD WORK IN YOU

Words and Music by
JON MOHR

I CAN SEE
(On the Emmaus Road)

Words by GLORIA GAITHER and DAVID MEECE
Music by DAVID MEECE

86

HOUSEHOLD OF FAITH

Words by BRENT LAMB
Music by JOHN ROSASCO

Male: Here we are, __ at the start, __ com-mit-ting to each oth- -er by His Word and from our hearts.

I REPENT

Words by DAVE NOEL
Music by STEVE GREEN and PHIL NAISH

LET US PRAISE THE ALMIGHTY

Words and Music by
J.D. MILLER

A MIGHTY FORTRESS

Words and Music by
MARTIN LUTHER
Arranged by Steve Green

Victoriously

A might-y for-tress is____ our God, A

bul-wark nev-er fail - ing. Our help-er He____ a -

mid____ the flood Of mor-tal ills pre-vail - ing. For

* *Accompaniment is optional.*

earth - ly pow'rs, No thanks to them, a - bid - eth. The

Spir - it and __ the gifts __ are ours, Through Him who with us

sid - eth. Let goods and kin - dred go, This

mor - tal life al - so. The bod - y they may

OH, I WANT TO KNOW YOU MORE

Words and Music by
STEVE FRY

Just the time I feel that _ I've been caught in the mire of
when my dai - ly feel deeds or - di - nar - i - ly lose _ life and

self, just the time I feel my _ mind's been bought _
song, my heart be - gins to bleed, sen - si - tiv - i - ty _____

PEOPLE NEED THE LORD

Words and Music by PHILL McHUGH
and GREG NELSON

SACRIFICE OF PRAISE

Words and Music by FRED MacKRELL
and PHIL NAISH

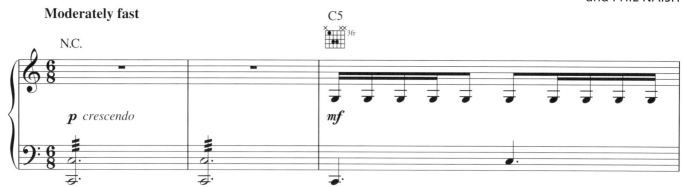

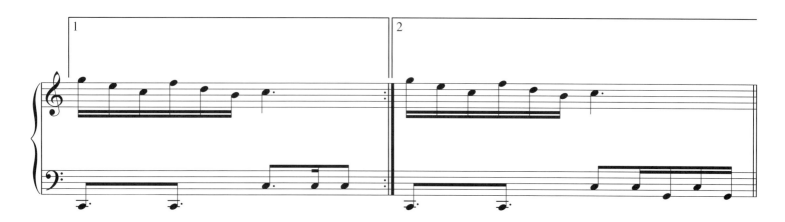

WE TRUST IN THE NAME OF THE LORD OUR GOD

Words and Music by
STEVEN CURTIS CHAPMAN

THAT'S WHERE HIS MERCY BEGINS

Words and Music by PHILL McHUGH,
GREG NELSON and SHANE KEISTER

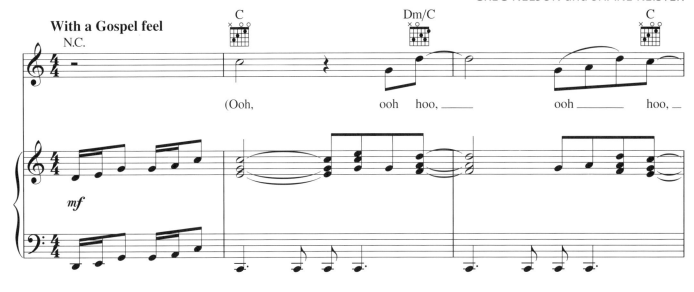

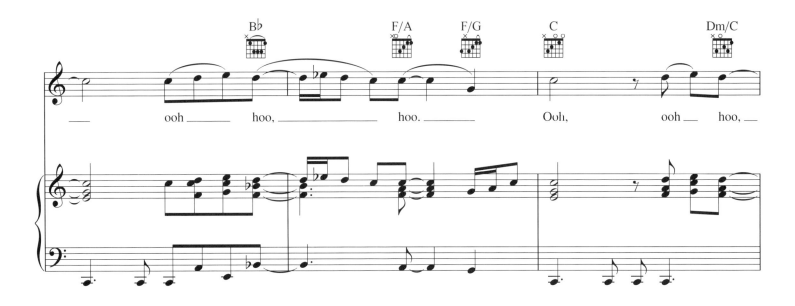

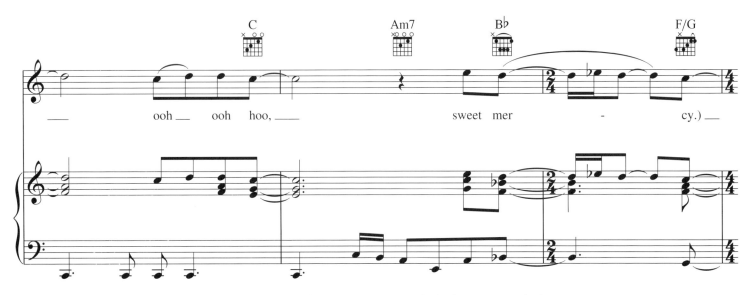

TOUCH YOUR PEOPLE ONCE AGAIN

Words and Music by
PELLE KARLSSON

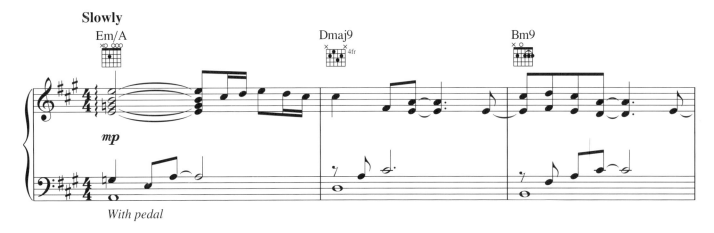

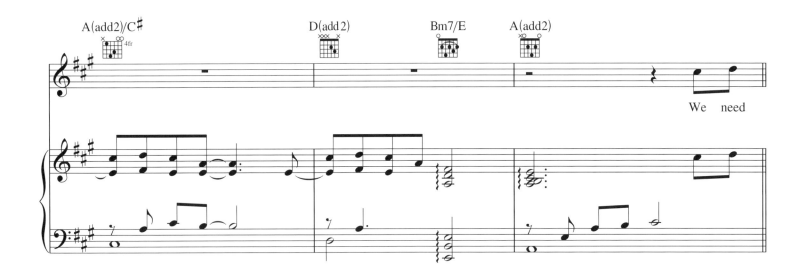

We need

wis - dom, __ we need pow - er, and true love __ for each oth - er; we have

see Your __ tired __ serv - ants and the bro - ken, __ wound - ed sol - diers. Oh, how

WE BELIEVE

Words and Music by DAN SCOTT
and NATHAN DIGESARE

WHAT WONDROUS LOVE IS THIS

Words and Music by
RONN HUFF

Slowly, with freedom

a cappella: What won- drous love is this, O my soul, O my

soul! What won- drous love is this, O my soul!

What won- drous love is this that _____

caused the Lord ___ of bliss to bear the dread- ful

curse for my soul, for my soul, to bear the dread- ful

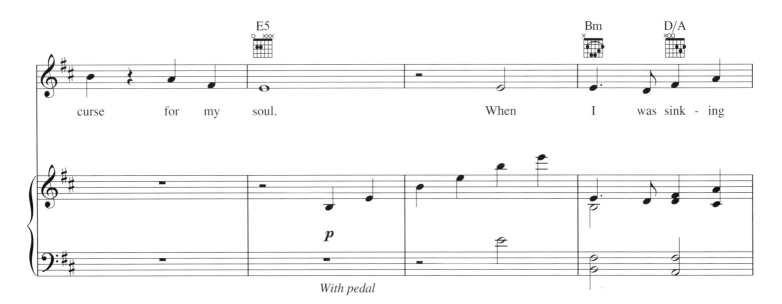

curse for my soul. When I was sink- ing

With pedal

WHEN HIS KINGDOM COMES

Words and Music by DOTTIE RAMBO
and DONY McGUIRE